If the Dead Could Sing

A Journal in Poetry

Elvira Borgstädt

Archway Publishing books may be ordered through booksellers or by contacting:

Archway Publishing
1663 Liberty Drive
Bloomington, IN 47403
www.archwaypublishing.com
1 (888) 242-5904

Because of the dynamic nature of the Internet, any web addresses or
links contained in this book may have changed since publication and
may no longer be valid. The views expressed in this work are solely those
of the author and do not necessarily reflect the views of the publisher,
and the publisher hereby disclaims any responsibility for them.

Any people depicted in stock imagery provided by Thinkstock are models,
and such images are being used for illustrative purposes only.
Certain stock imagery © Thinkstock.

ISBN: 978-1-4808-4993-8 (sc)
ISBN: 978-1-4808-4994-5 (e)

Library of Congress Control Number: 2017911224

Print information available on the last page.

Archway Publishing rev. date: 07/21/2017

observe

contemplate

transcend

Be content with what you have; rejoice in the way things are. When you realize there is nothing lacking, the whole world belongs to you.

—Lao Tzu

In memory of
Dr. Wayne W. Dyer
Leonard Cohen
Gwen Ifill

CONTENTS

Turn back to the higher planes and plunge into the cosmic ocean once again…

The human soul needs immensity, only in immensity can it be happy and feel free to breath.

—Omraam Mikhail Aivanhoy

FOREWORD

Elvira Borgstädt brings to these poems a sensibility that is both Midwestern and European, the plain, loving details of a Robert Bly restrained in the shadow of a stalking assassin who lingers nearby. Darkness hovers quietly over Borgstädt's observations: an unnamed, unacknowledged presence which subtly shifts everything and never leaves her company. Except for "Exoskeleton" she does not refer to multiple sclerosis — and she never honors it with a name, although it is out to destroy her.

In the movies, we have seen this before: an intense concentration on detail in the presence of overwhelming danger. We have *felt* it before by watching the desperate click of knitting needles as the killer approaches from behind. In the psychology of our television world, she is "in denial," and we urgently want her to turn around. But the heroine knows it is too late and wraps her arms around whatever she can.

Borgstädt denies nothing, having recognized the approaching beast years ago and with a clear-eyed understanding of its brutal path. So she turns her eyes away from it and embraces the moments, the details, the unexpected gifts in her daily life. The proximity of death does heighten the senses, calls us to measure what we will leave behind, and she gives us poems about the life which surrounds her own, as it recedes.

Borgstädt's quiet mysticism is informed by the teachings of the *Tao Te Ching* and the thinking of Meister Eckhard, the 13th Century Dominican monk and mystic, whom she studied in depth while a graduate student at the University of Chicago's Divinity School. Eckhard distinguished between a life of good works and a life of faith, which brought him to the attention of Church hierarchy preoccupied with detecting heresy. Likewise, Borgstädt's embrace of the physical and immediate directly challenges the certainty of multiple sclerosis. She beats the muffled drum for every living thing.

David Habercom
Boston

INTRODUCTION

And here it is. The book of poetry I have been meaning to write for some time. It seems a miracle that it unfolded so effortlessly when inspiration arose out of illness and brought me back to writing.

I had always envisioned growing old in good health, endowed with vitality and strength. After a productive life, I wanted to take my time retracing the ancient steps of Machu Picchu, visit the Valley of the Kings, walk the island of Shikoku with its 88 temples, and go on a walkabout in the Australian outback. In my adopted homeland, I meant to follow in the footsteps of John Muir, Ansel Adams, Georgia O'Keefe.

Instead, my life took a very different turn at forty-two, when the specter of paralysis invaded my busy life and changed everything. Multiple Sclerosis would force me to sit down and re-focus every aspect of my life.

As a child, I had witnessed this illness annihilate my beloved aunt Erika, and I was determined not to let this devil have its way with me. For more than two decades I fought it with all my might, became an MS expert without a medical degree. I mastered alternative treatments, nutrition, and physical therapy. But, as if to mock me, my immune system went into overdrive in a relentless assault on the myelin surrounding my nerves, on my spinal cord and brain. There were times when daily living became too difficult and an early death seemed the only answer.

It was during those dark hours that I truly faced my own mortality. For the first time in my life, the future drifted out of sight, and the present became my only reality. I wrestled with death and the heart wrenching fear that accompanies that struggle. In time the fear subsided, changed, and in the end, I learned to "love death" as did Pierre Bezukhov in Tolstoy's *War and Peace*.

So, dear reader, take from this book what you will, and be assured that in the very depth of suffering lies the golden path that leads us back to the eternal source from which everything springs.

Ehli Borgstädt
Wisconsin, USA 2017

OBSERVATION

Live in the sunshine, swim the sea, drink the wild air.

—*Ralph Waldo Emerson*

New Moon

Cool crescent
floating in
ebony sky.
Your promise
beckons the
silent woods.

Across the Room

You are asleep
jaw dropped, mouth
like a cavern
eyes in REM.

You dream of past glory,
the salt of your land,
your father's vineyards
your mother's bread.

All here, returned
in this house, at this moment
while a brilliant sky denies
the raging storm outside.

Metamorphosis

Backlit
by the sun,
these biting flyers
turn from menace
into splendor
in the sky.

Contrary to Nature

Contrary to nature
the oak leans north.

An inner wisdom inspires it away
from the sun

to steady its majestic frame
at the edge of the bluff.

Drought

Late summer and the crickets
chirp endlessly – insisting,
serenading the stagnant air.

Bone parching drought appeared
in Spring – stayed,
and stayed.

The soil is scorched
and everything yearns,
yearns for rain.

But harvest comes early.
Fruit is blemished and meager.
The fields yield no grain.

Only the wasps thrive,
ceaselessly nursing
their open hives.

Now – exposed and cold
in unforgiving autumn nights,
they grow greedy for life.

And I think of my mother
at ninety-five.

Upon Reading Verse 6 of the Tao

After a night of gentle rain
morning glitters the grass
with mica

and out of nowhere
five rabbits, now here,
perform a primal dance.

They run. They leap.
Somersaults
complete their chase,

all in a moment
of perfect
grace.

The Hollow Gourd

A wren inspects the nesting place,
a hollow gourd nestled
in the honey locust near the porch.

Last summer, I saw eight
little-ones pop
from its tiny opening.

Clumsy wings aflutter
into the hazelnut bush, and on
to the railing of the porch.

All eight, lined up
testing their wings.
All eight in unison

chattering, oblivious
to my watching
their coming of age.

The Fawn

A yearling doe
browses the rose bush
outside my window.
Delicate lips sample
the tender pink.

It is high noon.
She ambles outside the fence
settles under the young burr oak.

Just this morning
I saw her come from the woods
followed by a tiny fawn.

She seems content, chewing,
and I wonder where
in the tall prairie grass
has she hidden
the little one.

A Dragonfly

A dragonfly lands on my shoulder.
It glistens iridescent
in the sun.

I remember the first time
I saw one, while swimming
in Wolf Lake, decades ago.

It hovered slightly ahead
of my face, skimming
the soft ripples of water.

All the way across and back,
the steady hum of wings playing
its own rhapsody,

like a message.

Tao Harmony

A hummingbird visits
my open window.

At a distance
green jewels crowd the feeders
at dusk.

They drink deeply
while a breeze conquers
the heat of day.

Crickets make ready
to chirp the night
away.

Like Clockwork

The spider's web is woven.
Silken filaments, arranged
symmetrical and perfect,
confront me on the threshold
to the porch.

I disconnect the anchoring thread,
move it gently to the side
that my stepping out
will not disturb
her morning meal.

Fireflies

Restless they flash
signals in the dark,
while a full moon sits
pregnant in the treetops.

Nights like these
reveal their multitudes,
when meadows explode
in fireworks.

With perfect purpose
these June fliers
weave a tapestry
of living light.

My Hummingbird Perches

My hummingbird perches
on the naked branch.
For years she has returned
to build her tiny nest inside this bush,
a Hazelnut, beside the porch.
She sits alert
surveys her surroundings.
Then preens herself, meticulous
the wings inside and out,
then the tail, splayed to its full glory.
And last, she cranes her neck
up high, for the long bill
to reach her chest and back.
I've watched this ritual before,
and every time
I recognize the miracle
that brings her back
to raise her young
right here.

My Summer Guest Sings the Dawn Away

He serenades the secluded sun
sitting in the Honey Locust
hidden from sight by tiny leaves.

He calls—he mocks—he chirps
and sings
his repertory boundless.

Each morning the sun emerges
and together we beseech
the coming day.

Rain Lilies

Pink stars–petals open
seeking the sun.
They welcome the slender beak
probing deep
to feed her young.

Distinctive chirp and hum of wings
tell me my humming friend is near.
She is too fast to catch in flight,
but when she hovers above
a chosen bloom, I see
her perfect form.

She is pure grace as she moves
from one to another,
never skipping
a single blossom.

At the Birdbath

Perched on trumpet vine,
the yellow finch
contemplates
the end of summer.

Grackles

Blustering in
like large
leaves
driven
by purpose,
scouring
the ground.
Their heads
and necks
glisten
iridescent
blue
in the cool
autumn sun.

Autumn

Fat squirrel sits
under the white oak
munching acorns.

Waiting for the Green

Silence explodes,
a cacophony of snow geese
call from the river.

It is too early—ice
will blanket the water again,
but the flock gathers with the call.

In a flurry of wings, lift off
north bound, to etch
a perfect V into the sky.

It is too early, but even
from this distance
I see leaves reflect the sun

in ten-thousand shades of green.
A green that sooths the eye
and calms the mind.

Abundance curbs my hunger
in the fertile green,
where all is satisfied.

CONTEMPLATION

Truly, it is in the darkness that one finds the light, so when we are in sorrow, then this light is nearest of all to us.

—Meister Eckhart

Full Moon

Gleaming lantern, hung low
above the water, you paint the river
with light–throwing shadows
into hushed woods.

Forty Years On

Forty years on
I see you in the doorway
unchanged, smiling.
Your voice points back
to another time.

Recollection
infuses my air
with the perfume of home,
a heady scent
almost forgotten.

Once it was easy
to hold you, but not now,
as you tender your gifts
of serenity, of kindness,
of love.

Exoskeleton

What I need
is full body-armor
worn like a skin.

Bones are strong,
but legs won't balance
the body anymore.

What I need are nerves ready
to relay my command,
for the signals
to reach their destination.

An exoskeleton,
a network of fibers, conduits of carbon
the strength of muscle
over bone.

Yet most of all,
what I need
is the guts
to go on.

Bear

Arthritic and half lame,
my beloved Chow
leads me outside.
Down the driveway,
he stops.
I watch and wait.
When he resumes
we hug the autumn prairie's edge.
Press on,
at the edge of the woods
to the log fence
along the bluff.
Here we rest,
look down on the once-
mighty Mississippi.
How the waters have slowed
and islands have sprung
from the usual flood.
He stands, testing the breeze.
Finally, he turns his head.
His knowing eyes meet mine
and we walk,
along the log fence

to the eastern woods.
Up the hill
to a fork in the path.
He pauses with indecision.
Into the prairie
or turn home?
And we go back,
ever so slowly.
He takes in the sun,
the crickets,
and for the last time
the fragrant earth.

Elegy for Neda Agha Sultan

Iran 2009

Neda,
your death comes to me live
over the internet.
Your eyes complete
the arc toward death
as men lower you
to the pavement.

Your father cries out
while another tells you
to hold on,
but your eyes roll
slowly from left to right
and your life-blood,
red and fierce,
pours like a river
from your mouth.

Neda,
you came to protest
in peace
within a crowd,

where the sniper's bullet
found you.

Your shock is palatable.
Your innocence prevails.
May your death be remembered.
May your blood
feed a river of rage.
May your sacrifice
call justice
to your land.

Elke Paula Borgstädt

1957-2014

The woods are naked
after a blaze of yellows
orange and red.

The trees have shed
everything, and the dead
are silent.

Fresh are my sister's ashes
on a mantelpiece, kept by a husband
who could not let her go.

So the suffering went on too long.
But now it is done, and the earth
again smells sweet.

On a Thursday in September

On a Thursday in September
your journey ended at dawn,
my daughter at your side.

I woke from a restless night, too early
for light to creep over the horizon
and like a blade in my heart
I felt your struggle.

With morning came the call,
you were gone. Relief swept the air.
The sunburst forth
and I knew you were not alone.

"Dying is a hard business" you told her
when she arrived, to shepherd you safely
to the other side.

Here You Are

Here you are—suddenly
in a gust of wind
hitting my window.

Startled I look up from my book, and see
the young oak illuminated
by dazzling light.

Last year's leaves
red and dry
still cling to the tree,
and in a blaze
the sun erases winter.

It was your wish, spoken softly,
that I remember you in the wind.
And here you are

after months of silence,
calling me to the tree
that bears witness.

Reincarnation

How else can a newborn child
turn her head to lock eyes with me,
through a camera, thousands of miles away
as if to say:

"Sister I am here"

I Am at Ease

I am at ease
as I remember the infant
at my breast, suckling with delight,
her small hands caressing
my face.

How she takes my breast
into her hands,
yanks it from her mouth, milk flying
and with a squeal
she stuffs the nipple back
to suckle again.

And I remember the toddler
hiding in the stairway,
to reveal herself
only after
my panicked search.

And I remember my little girl at daycare
who does not nap,
until they play Vivaldi:
The Four Seasons.

Waiting for a Clivia to Bloom Yellow

The gift was made
but the seedling had no strength.

After years of nurture
it has grown bent
at the base,
yet leaves grow stronger.

As I wait for the yellow
globe of blossoms,

I am soothed
by the brilliant orange
of the prolific bloomer, received
some time ago

from my daughter,
when she still thought of me.

And Now Silence

For Vanessa

I remember my years
balanced on the edge, gazing
into an abyss too deep to fathom.
How after years of struggle
there was nothing left.

And now that I have jumped
her loss has been a mystery.
Floating, I have entered
a world of zero gravity.

Once told that "a painful end
is better than pain without an end"

I find that truth deep in my gut
where a fierce pebble replaced
that throbbing pain.

She Reflects

She reflects on how she failed
her own mother.

Sadness and grief
haunt her nights

and sleepless
she regrets

her own failing.
A callous disregard

of an old woman's wish
to come home.

Now at ninety-nine she knows
the pain of separation,

and in her dreams
she begs forgiveness
for something
she did not understand,

till now.

TRANSFORMATION

We shall not cease from exploration
and the end of all our exploring
will be to arrive where we started,
and know the place for the first time.

—*T.S. Elliot*

Waning Moon

Songs end
and crickets die.
A waning
sliver of gold
tucks deep into
the somber fabric
of autumn sky.

If the Dead Could Sing

Would we hear odes of joy?
Would the songs tell of a better place?
If the dead could speak,
would they ask forgiveness
for past transgressions?
Would they show new insight?
Would the meaning of life
have changed?

Would my father, dead
in mid-life, have tamed his anger?
Would he have seen
that all along, there was a better way?
And if he had,
would it make a difference
now?

And my green-eyed sister,
dead at sixty-two,

would she regret her separation?
Self-imposed and cold.
Would the son she raised in isolation,
have grasped our love,
now lost forever?

If the dead could speak
would they tell us
of a kinder place?
Where ego has no grip
on them, on us?
Where reflection leads
to understanding?

And my youngest sister, dead
by a cancer that ate her alive.
Would she tell me
that in the end, her fear
of dying dissolved,
was bogus
like a counterfeit?

When the Body Dreams

Agony drops away, and I enter
the salty expanse,
an ocean of primal joy.
My snout pierces heaving waves,
dorsal fin and flippers sprout
from glistening trunk.
A tailfin grows,
propels me through turbulent
currents of blue.
I leap from the waves
arc back and join the pod,
we chatter, we are the hunt.

When the body dreams perfection
I rise from my bed of sorrow.
Slow motion, undulating arms,
effortless, the torso lifts,
spine straightens,
and my face turns
to the sun.
I am a dancer, the cloak of despair
falls away like sand.
I turn, and turn,

move with unyielding grace.
I am absolved, forgiven, pardoned.

When the body dreams,
a bald eagle soars into the sky.
Sun glistens my wings, air
thermals lift me. Unruffled feathers
grant me flight, and I glide,
I play the wind. A sibling calls
prey clutched in ruthless claws.
She releases her kill
and we toss the fish like a ball
and catch, in the currents of effortless joy.
Here all is one, one form,
one life.

Such ease, when the body
dreams perfection, dreams,
and leaves it all behind.

Nightly

Nightly
the dream recurs
and I walk again.

Lao-tzu Bids Me

Lao-tzu bids me
to be like water,
formless and soft,
flowing down to the valley,
to merge into that great ocean
of selfless joy.

He speaks of
a coming together, of all
that have shed ego,
all who have followed the way
to oneness, to nothingness,
to pure joy.

Let Forgiveness Clear the Path

Let my sadness flow out
and the void be filled
with love.

Let the Mother of all things
reach out and show me
the way.

The Way

The frayed umbilical has stabilized.
It grew from fragile cord
of flickering mica
into a cascade,
pulsing and alive.

Now the goal
is to explore the *Tao*.
Back to that, which is
formless and perfect,
empty and serene,
unchanging and infinite.

Back to the eternally present,
ever flowing source of the Divine.
And now, that I know the way,
I find a two-way path.

Going Home

I step onto the path.
Pulsing energy
enters my feet,
moves upward.
Balance returns,
I put away my canes.

I see the river of light,
hear the music
of the *Tao*.

The weight I carry
drops from my limbs,
my heart beats
a new rhythm.
Abundance returns.

Suffering falls away,
dissolves, disappears
like the mist, consumed
into the rising sun.

The Work is Done

Going home I step
across the threshold of light.

The Mother of all things
takes my hand,

and I walk the shining path.
Each step brings me closer, peace

surrounds me like a summer breeze.
Love flows into me,

recognition bursts upon me,
and my body dissolves.

I merge with the source,
I am that I am.

For the Raindrop

For the raindrop
joy is entering the river.

And for me, joy
is entering the great silence.

Death Without Death

Can I reach for the spark, that ignites
in a dream I do not understand?
Take hold of its essence?
Grasp what awakens, what has slumbered,
in the fullness of time?

With trepidation, I watch the child
climb into a sphere.
See the orb expand around him,
and close into a gleaming shell.

The child describes explosions,
a white essence filling the void.
His voice grows weaker,
fades, is silent.

I panic, rip open the globe.
Find nothing remain of the child.
Nothing, but a chalice
of pure light.

Dreamtime

A didgeridoo wails across the desert.
Our trek into the hills takes long.
Finally, we reach the pueblo.

Laid out perfectly,
these rooms housed ancestors,
back in time.

I come to my room and find
two perfect vessels
large and round,

the potter's hands still evident.
I am in awe, sit in silence,
reach for the essence.

Without a touch
the ancient vessels lose their brilliance,
split in two, and fall.

As if to say
the time of abundance
has passed.

Encounter

Morning dew reveals
the intricate weave
of spider-webs.

Shimmering droplets weigh
on diaphanous fiber.

The webs hang everywhere,
the air is heavy with mist.

The bluffs,
the Mississippi, and Iowa,
have disappeared.

She comes to me
in the last dream of the night.

Love burst forth like a fatal brilliance.
Lava, bubbling in slow motion,
in searing red.
I feel her innocence,
she is vulnerable,
in need of shelter.

I wake and urgency washes over me.
I call, hear her hesitant voice.

Find her cautious happiness,
her rushed conversation.

She swims in the details of life,
focused on things,
as if they were real.

I draw back, sensing that in time
she will learn to look deeper.

In time, she will
catch the hidden truth.

The Parting

She came to me a decade ago
feral and shy
small and nimble
like an arctic fox of pure white.

Eyes rimed by charcoal
fixed vigilantly
on my every move.

Her gaze went deep,

and after ten years
of unconditional love
she died in my arms,
and we parted, for now.

Today, on a day of autumn mist,
undulating in brilliant shades of gray,
out of no-where
a white finch
appears on the bird bath.

Perching silently, coal rimmed eyes
fixed in my direction.
It bows its head in greeting,

and speaks to me of nothingness.

Origami

For Doris

As it turns out
in the beginning
everything is folded like paper:

Oak leaves
and butterfly wings
a cricket's leg
an elephant's ear
the skin of a snake
the breath of a dragon.

Folded
like dark matter,
the lattice
on which cosmic dust solidified,
clumped, and grew
into highways of starlight.

From there to here,
what does it matter
if I am a bird in the sky,

a part of the flock
that shoots from the woods,
scouring for food.

Or earthbound,
a creature of uncounted folds
like the earthworm,
digging my way through heavy soil.

Soft folds of flesh, burrowing
through darkness,
leaving tunnels in my wake,
like highways.

Come My Beloved

For Gheorghe

Let us bury the dead,
erase their sorrow from the land,
and suspend the memory of their suffering.

Let us stride over the mountains,
bathe in the ocean of a new life,
and from the silence of winter call forth the sun.

Let us build a new home
where recollection fills rooms,
but regret finds neither place, nor time.

Let us dream a new dream
where the earth is brimming with riches,
but greed has neither grip,
    nor power, nor persuasion.

Let us grow benevolence in our hearts,
revere the rain in its abundance,
and share the plethora of the land.

Let the *Tao* teach us, and the divine
Mother show us the place
where miracles are manifest.

Even God Requires Breath

For Nick

When we tame the greedy beast,
sorrow lifts, and we are free to sail
the ocean of our agile minds.
We reach into immensity,
explore the island of contentment,
grow the crops of peace,
and harvest the sun.

When breath comes easy,
we dance in the aura of angels,
fit through the eye of a needle,
step onto the land
where horizons have no limits,
where reality is open-ended,
where the impossible exists.

When we surrender our weapons,
war ends, and the beast is lulled
into a deep, abiding sleep.

Peace heals all wounds
and the wolfs of violence are content.
All that, in a new existence
where even God requires breath.

ACKNOWLEDGEMENTS

I would like to thank the wonderful people who made it possible for this book to see the light of day:

David Habercom who graciously took the lead in editing, and Susan Scarlata, whose comments helped refine the manuscript and turn it into a book. My husband Gheorghe Tinghili who stood by me and made my life so much better with his loving care. Garin Aglietti, whose dedication to ease suffering enabled me to endure. My friends, MaryAnn Shultz who encouraged me to write, Linda Johll who kept my home spick-and-span, and Julie Esser who never tired of lending me a helping hand; and especially my grandson Nicolas Broske, whose weekly skype visits kept me on track to see it through.